D1561965

DAVID COTTRELL'S
COLLECTION OF
FAVORITE
QUOTATIONS

Words to
Inspire, Motivate & Encourage

DAVID COTTRELL'S
COLLECTION OF
FAVORITE
QUOTATIONS

Words to

Inspire, Motivate & Encourage

Inquiries regarding permission for use of the material contained in this book should be addressed to:

CornerStone Leadership Institute
P.O. Box 764087
Dallas, TX 75376
888.789.LEAD

Printed in the United States of America
ISBN: 0-9788137-2-3

Credits

Design, art direction and production	Melissa Monogue, Back Porch Creative info@BackPorchCreative.com

TABLE OF CONTENTS

INTRODUCTION

A short saying oft contains much wisdom.
– Sophocles

I love quotations. I marvel at those who can take a complex subject and express it in a couple of sentences ... in a way I can remember.

Quotes are powerful. They help us to learn from the past, understand the present, and prepare for the future.

This collection of my favorite quotations is compiled to reinforce the principles of ***12 Choices ... That Lead to Your Success***. Many of the quotes are from famous people who have helped shape the world. Others are from friends and business associates. Still others are from people I've never heard of. Regardless of the source, each quote was selected to inspire, motivate, and encourage you.

May the timeless wisdom this book contains provide you with the courage to make choices that will lead to your greatest success!

PART ONE

THE CHARACTER CHOICES ...
THE FOUNDATION OF SUCCESS.

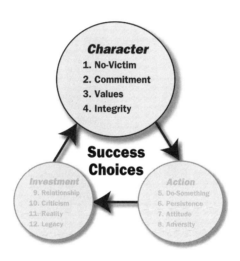

*"Character is the foundation upon which one must
build to win respect. Just as no worthy building
can be erected on a weak foundation,
so no lasting reputation worthy of respect
can be built on a weak character."*

– R.C. Samsel

THE NO-VICTIM CHOICE ...
DON'T LET YOUR PAST EAT YOUR FUTURE

When you become the victim, you give up the right to create your future and allow yourself to be buffeted by what life brings.

In every situation, whether in your work life or your personal life, there are always choices – if you choose to see them. If you choose to put on the blinders of victimization, prepare to accept the disappointments that come when you fail to achieve the success you deserve.

Never be bullied into silence. Never allow yourself to be made a victim. Accept no one's definition of your life, but define yourself.
— *Harvey S. Firestone*

Things turn out best for the people who make the best of the way things turn out.

— *John Wooden*

Life can only be understood backwards, but it must be lived forward.
— *Soren Kierkegaard*

We live in the present, we dream of the future, but we learn eternal truths from the past.
— *Madame Chiang Kai-shek*

If you are going to fulfill your destiny, you gotta get in the game, you gotta stay in the game, and you gotta follow the game plan.
— *Billy Cox*

Living in the past is a dull and lonely business; looking back strains the neck muscles, causes you to bump into people not going your way.
— *Edna Ferber*

The worst thing you can do is to try to cling to something that's gone, or to recreate it.
— *Johnette Napolitano*

The good old days were never that good, believe me. The good new days are today, and better days are coming tomorrow. Our greatest songs are still unsung.
— *Hubert H. Humphrey*

It is not what happens that determines the major part of your future. What happens, happens to us all. It is what you do about what happens that counts.
— *Jim Rohn*

Your past is important, but it is not nearly as important to your present as is the way you see your future.
— *Dr. Tony Campolo*

We are free up to the point of choice, then the choice controls the chooser.

– Mary Crowley

Life will be to a large extent what we ourselves make of it.

– Samuel Smiles

Of all sad words of tongue or pen, the saddest are these: It might have been.

– John Greenleaf Whittier

Destiny is not a matter of chance, it is a matter of choice; it is not a thing to be waited for, it is a thing to be achieved.

– William Jennings Bryan

Life's rewards go to those who let their actions rise above their excuses.

– Lee J. Colan

A man carries his success or failure with him …
it does not depend on outside conditions.
— Ralph Waldo Trine

———————

Do what you can, with what you have, where
you are.
— Theodore Roosevelt

———————

Forgive yourself for your faults and your
mistakes and move on.
— Les Brown

———————

If you want to be miserable, think about
yourself, about what you want, what you like,
what respect people ought to pay you and
what people think of you.
— Charles Kingsley

———————

Victory has a thousand fathers; defeat is
an orphan.
— Confucius

———————

I used to say, 'I sure hope things will change.'
Then I learned that the only way things are
going to change for me is when I change.

— *Jim Rohn*

**Success means doing the best
we can with what we have.
Success is in the doing, not
the getting — in the trying,
not the triumph.**

— *Wynn Davis*

The greatest power that a person possesses is
the power to choose.

— *J. Martin Kohe*

People are always blaming their circumstances
for what they are. The people who get on in
this world are they who get up and look for
the circumstances they want, and, if they can't
find them, make them.

— *George Bernard Shaw*

When you blame others, you give up your power to change.

— *Anonymous*

We are taught you must blame your father, your sisters, your brothers, the school, the teachers — you can blame anyone, but never blame yourself. It's never your fault. But it's always your fault, because if you want to change, you're the one who has got to change. It's as simple as that, isn't it?

— *Katharine Hepburn*

One's philosophy is not best expressed in words; it's expressed in the choices one makes. In the long run we shape our lives and we shape ourselves. The process never ends until we die. And the choices we make are ultimately our responsibility.

— *Eleanor Roosevelt*

THE COMMITMENT CHOICE ...
BE PASSIONATE ENOUGH TO SUCCEED

Don't allow the fear of failure to cause you to fail.

It's easy to talk about commitment, but commitment is more than words. It's a choice, an attitude and a passion to achieve success, whatever the price.

Commitment is about doing what you say you'll do ... when you say you'll do it. It's about under-promising or over-delivering. It's about being kind to yourself when you fall short … and it's about believing failure is moving you one step closer to success.

When work, commitment and pleasure all become one and you reach that deep well where passion lives, nothing is impossible.
— *Anonymous*

Destiny is not a matter of chance, it is a matter of choice; it is not a thing to be waited for, it is a thing to be achieved.
— *Williams Jennings Bryan*

If you don't make a total commitment to whatever you're doing, then you start looking to bail out the first time the boat starts leaking. It's tough enough getting that boat to shore with everybody rowing, let alone when a guy stands up and starts putting his life jacket on.
— *Lou Holtz*

If a man is called to be a street sweeper, he should sweep streets even as Michelangelo painted, or Beethoven composed music, or Shakespeare wrote poetry. He should sweep streets so well that all the hosts of heaven and earth will pause to say, here lived a great street sweeper who did his job well.

— *Martin Luther King, Jr.*

The average person puts only 25% of his energy and ability into his work. The world takes off its hat to those who put in more than 50% of their capacity, and stands on its head for those few-and-far-between souls who devote 100%.

— *Andrew Carnegie*

Standing in the middle of the road is very dangerous; you get knocked down by traffic from both sides.

— *Margaret Thatcher*

If you don't love what you do, you have two choices: You can either change what you're doing, or you can change what you love.

— *Billy Cox*

I can tell you how to get what you want: You've just got to keep a thing in view and go for it and never let your eyes wander to right or left or up or down. And looking back is fatal.
— *William J. Locke*

Passion exposes possibilities.
— *Lee J. Colan*

Make a clear, unequivocal decision to be the best, and don't leave yourself any 'outs.' Tell yourself, 'I'm going to do it.' That's it. Period.
— *Billy Cox*

Unhappiness is best defined as the difference between our talents and our expectations.
— *Edward de Bono*

To be successful, you have to have your heart in your business and your business in your heart.
— *Thomas Watson, Sr.*

Be like a postage stamp. Stick to one thing until you get there.

— *Josh Billings*

One might as well try to ride two horses moving in different directions, as to try to maintain, in equal force, two opposing or contradictory sets of desires.

— *Robert Collier*

The tragedy of life doesn't lie in not reaching your goal. The tragedy lies in having no goal to reach.

— *Benjamin Mays*

Many are stubborn in pursuit of the path they have chosen, few in pursuit of the goal.

— *Friedrich Nietzsche*

I'm a great believer in luck, and I find that harder I work, the more of it I have.

— *Thomas Jefferson*

The world stands aside to let anyone pass who knows where he is going.

— *David Starr Jordan*

Thunder is good. Thunder is impressive. But it is the lightning that does the work.

— *Mark Twain*

The happiness of a man in this life does not consist in the absence, but in the mastery, of his passions.

— *Alfred Lord Tennyson*

The mind is a bit like a garden. If it isn't fed and cultivated, weeds will take it over.

— *Erwin G. Hall*

There is one quality that one must possess to win, and that is definiteness of purpose — the knowledge of what one wants and a burning desire to possess it.

— *Napoleon Hill*

No one is compelled to serve great causes unless he feels fit for it, but nothing is more certain than you cannot take the lead in great causes as a half timer.

— *Winston Churchill*

There is no passion to be found in playing small — in settling for a life that is less than what you are capable of living.

— *Nelson Mandela*

The quality of a person's life is in direct proportion to their commitment to excellence, regardless of their chosen field of endeavor.

— *Vince Lombardi*

It takes more than three weeks to prepare a good impromptu speech.

— *Mark Twain*

I cannot teach anybody anything; I can only make them think.

— *Socrates*

It is not enough to have a good mind. The main thing is to use it well.

— *Rene Descartes*

If you want to be successful, know what you are doing, love what you are doing and believe in what you are doing.

— *Will Rogers*

Hard work spotlights the character of people: some turn up their sleeves, some turn up their noses, and some don't turn up at all.

— *Sam Ewig*

The best prize life offers is the chance to work hard at work worth doing.

— *Theodore Roosevelt*

Decide what you want, decide what you are willing to exchange for it, establish your priorities, and go to work!

— H. Lamar Hunt

You only have to solve two problems when going to the moon: first, how to get there; and second, how to get back. The key is don't leave until you have solved both problems.

— Neil Armstrong

If you can dream it, you can do it. Never lose sight of the fact that this whole thing was started by a mouse.

— Walt Disney

Many men go fishing all of their lives without knowing that it is not fish they are after.

— Henry David Thoreau

THE VALUES CHOICE ...

CHOOSING THE RIGHT ENEMIES

Enemies are a by-product of success.

Choosing the right enemies?

Indeed, for those who are successful in achieving their goals, enemies are a by-product of your success. The key to successfully dealing with your enemies is being able to identify who they are and understanding why they have chosen to become your enemy.

Does this mean successful people should be paranoid? No, it means that you have a crystal clear understanding of your values. It also means being strong enough to maintain your values regardless of the situation.

Never sacrifice your values to accommodate your enemies!

A wise man learns more from his enemies than a fool from his friends.
— *Baltasar Gracian*

Every beginning is a consequence. Every beginning ends something.
— *Paul Valery*

There is a time when we must firmly choose the course we will follow, or the relentless drift of events will make the decision for us.
— *Herbert B. Prochnow*

You can please all of the people some of the time and some of the people all the time, but you cannot please all the people all the time.
— *Abraham Lincoln*

Associate yourself with men of good quality if you esteem your own reputation, for 'tis better to be alone than in bad company.
— *George Washington*

You shall judge a man by his foes as well as by his friends.
— *Joseph Conrad*

There is no little enemy.
— *Benjamin Franklin*

Do not judge, or you too will be judged. For in the same way you judge others, you will be judged, and with the measure you use, it will be measured to you.
— *Matthew 7: 1-2*

Forgive your enemies, but never forget their names.

— *John F. Kennedy*

To be wronged is nothing unless you continue to remember it.

— *Confucius*

The only thing necessary for the triumph of evil is for good men to do nothing.

— *Edmund Burke*

Faith in oneself ... is the best and safest course.

— *Michelangelo*

Always forgive your enemies — nothing annoys them so much.

— *Oscar Wilde*

If we could read the secret history of our enemies, we should find in each man's life sorrow and suffering enough to disarm all hostility.

— *Henry Wadsworth Longfellow*

In order to be irreplaceable, one must always be different.

— *Coco Chanel*

Don't carry a grudge. While you're carrying the grudge, the other guy's out dancing.

— *Buddy Hackett*

The only people with whom you should try to get even are those who have helped you.

— *Mae Maloo*

Conformity is the jailer of freedom and the enemy of growth.

— *John F. Kennedy*

I don't know the key to success, but the key to failure is trying to please everybody.

— *Bill Cosby*

You can straighten a worm, but the crook is in him and only waiting.

— *Mark Twain*

Those who earn promotions should prepare
for lost friendships among co-workers who
were not promoted as fast as they were.
— *Ken Carnes*

Love your enemies, for they shall tell you all
your faults.

— *Benjamin Franklin*

I have found that the greatest help in meeting
any problem with decency and self-respect and
whatever courage is demanded, is to know
where you yourself stand. That is, to have in
words what you believe and are acting from.
— *William Faulkner*

Instead of loving your enemies, treat your friends a little better.
— *Edgar Watson Howe*

Friends come and go, enemies linger.

— *Anonymous*

Keeping score of old scores and scars, getting even and one-upping, always make you less than you are.

— *Malcolm Forbes*

Keep away from people who try to belittle your ambition. Small people always do that, but the really great make you feel that you, too, can become great.

— *Mark Twain*

Wounds from a friend can be trusted, but an enemy multiplies kisses.

— *Proverbs 27:6*

THE INTEGRITY CHOICE ...
DOING THE RIGHT THING

*Integrity is never being ashamed
of your reflection.*

Without a doubt, your personal integrity is your most prized possession. Our integrity is constantly tested, and we have an opportunity to prove it or lose it with every decision we make.

The choice of integrity – doing the right thing – is one of the most important choices you can make.

Doing the right thing is not always the easiest thing to do – but it is always the right thing to do. Choosing to do the right thing – even when it's painful – ensures you will maintain your most precious possession throughout your personal and professional journey.

There is no pillow as soft as a clear conscience.
— *John Wooden*

Integrity is telling myself the truth, and honesty is telling the truth to other people.
— *Spencer Johnson*

A good name is more desirable than great riches; to be esteemed is better than silver or gold.
— *Proverbs 22:1*

Anyone who thinks they can go to the top and stay there without being honest is dumb.
— *Mortimer Feinberg*

What lies behind us and what lies before us are tiny matters compared to what lies within us.
— *Ralph Waldo Emerson*

It is better to be defeated on principle than to win on lies.
— *Arthur Calwell*

There are always two choices. Two paths to take. One is easy. And its only reward is that it's easy.
— *Anonymous*

If you believe in unlimited quality and act in all your business dealings with total integrity, the rest will take care of itself.
— *Frank Perdue*

Integrity is not a 90 percent thing, not a 95 percent thing; either you have it or you don't.
— *Peter Scotese*

Character is like a tree and reputation like its shadow. The shadow is what we think of it — the real thing is the tree.
— *Abraham Lincoln*

One of the most striking differences between a cat and a lie is that a cat has only nine lives.
— *Mark Twain*

Truth has no special time of its own. Its hour is now — always.
— *Albert Schweitzer*

Integrity is the commitment to do what is right regardless of the circumstances — no hidden agendas, no political games. Do the right thing, period.
— *Ken Carnes*

The time is always right to do what is right.
— *Martin Luther King, Jr.*

Hold yourself responsible for a higher standard than anyone else expects of you. Never excuse yourself.

— Henry Ward Beecher

I know of no more encouraging fact than the unquestionable ability of man to elevate his life by a conscious endeavor.

— Henry David Thoreau

Success is simple. Do what's right, the right way, at the right time.

— Arnold Glasow

It is no use walking anywhere to preach unless our walking is our preaching.

— St. Francis of Assisi

With courage you will dare to take risks, have the strength to be compassionate and the wisdom to be humble. Courage is the foundation of integrity.

— Keshavan Nair

Character cannot be developed in ease and quiet. Only through experiences of trial and suffering can the soul be strengthened, vision cleared, ambition inspired and success achieved.
– *Helen Keller*

There are four ways, and only four ways, in which we have contact with the world. We are evaluated and classified by these four contacts: what we do, how we look, what we say, and how we say it.
– *Dale Carnegie*

Don't compromise yourself; you are all you've got.
– *Betty Ford*

Until you make peace with who you are, you'll never be content with what you have.
– *Doris Mortman*

The truth of the matter is that you always know the right thing to do. The hard part is doing it.
– *Norman Schwarzkopf*

No man has a good enough memory to make
a successful liar.

> — *Abraham Lincoln*

It takes less time to do a right thing than to
explain why you did it wrong.

> — *Henry Wadsworth Longfellow*

In matters of style, swim with the current; in
matters of principle, stand like a rock.

> — *Thomas Jefferson*

If you don't stand for something, you'll fall
for anything.

> — *Anonymous*

Courage is contagious. When a brave man takes a
stand, the spines of others are often stiffened.

> — *Billy Graham*

Even if you should suffer for what is right, you
are blessed.

> — *1 Peter 3:14*

A lie gets halfway around the world before the truth has a chance to get its pants on.
                        — *Winston Churchill*

———————————

Always do right. This will gratify some people and astonish the rest.
                        — *Mark Twain*

———————————

To see what is right and not to do it is cowardice.
                        — *Confucius*

———————————

In everything set them an example by doing what is good. In your teaching show integrity, seriousness, and soundness of speech that cannot be condemned, so that those who oppose you may be ashamed because they have nothing bad to say about us.
                        — *Titus 2: 7-8*

———————————

There can be no happiness if the things we believe in are different from the things we do.
                        — *Freya Stark*

———————————

PART TWO

THE ACTION CHOICES ...
THE MOVEMENT TOWARD SUCCESS.

*"A man is the sum of his actions,
of what he has done, of what he can do.
Nothing else."*

– Mahatma Gandhi

THE DO-SOMETHING CHOICE ...
DON'T VACATION ON SOMEDAY ISLE

Winners keep winning because they keep doing the necessary 'somethings' to win.

We all know people who have intentions of "doing something someday." It could be building a dream house, writing a book, navigating a sailboat, or moving forward in a relationship.

Intentions do not accomplish anything. Eventually you have to decide to quit intending and begin doing. It could begin today. It could begin right now. If you're not happy about how things are, choose to do something about it. For a better tomorrow, do something different today.

Someday Isle is not a dream vacation spot. It is an imaginary destination to which you will never arrive. It is the carrot on the stick perpetually in front of you. So close you can see it, yet you will never reach it. Don't vacation on Someday Isle.

— *Frank F. Lunn*

If you think you're too small to have an impact, try going to bed with a mosquito in the room.

— *Dame Anita Roddick*

Everyone who got where he is had to begin where he was.

— *Robert Louis Stevenson*

Don't wait. The time will never be just right. Start where you stand and work with whatever tools you may have at your command and better tools will be found as you go along.
— *Napoleon Hill*

Having the world's best idea will do you no good unless you act on it. People who want milk shouldn't sit on a stool in the middle of a field in hopes that a cow will back up to them.
— *Curtis Grant*

The pain of regret for not being prepared for an opportunity will last far longer than the pleasure of today's laziness.
— *Bryan Dodge*

Why not go out on a limb? That's where the fruit is.
— *Will Rogers*

You are the same today you'll be in five years
except for two things: the people you meet
and the books you read.

— *Charlie "Tremendous" Jones*

**Everyone who has ever taken
a shower has an idea. It's the
person who gets out of the
shower, dries off and does
something about it who
makes a difference.**

— *Nolan Bushnell*

Decision is a sharp knife that cuts clean and
straight. Indecision is a dull one that hacks and
tears and leaves ragged edges behind.

— *Jan McKeithen*

Opportunity rarely knocks on your door.
Knock rather on opportunity's door if you
ardently wish to enter.

— *B.C. Forbes*

How far would Moses have gone if he had taken a poll in Egypt?
> *– Harry Truman*

Opportunities multiply as they are seized.
> *– John Wicker*

Waiting is a trap. There will always be reasons to wait. The truth is, there are only two things in life, reasons and results, and reasons simply don't count.
> *– Robert Anthony*

Now that it's all over, what did you do yesterday that's worth mentioning?
> *– Coleman Cox*

One of the marks of successful people is that they are action-oriented. One of the marks of average people is that they are talk-oriented.
> *– Brian Tracy*

To open a book brings profit.
> *– Garry Kinder*

Often the difference between a successful man and a failure is not one's better abilities or ideas, but the courage that one has to bet on one's ideas, to take a calculated risk – and to act.

– *Maxwell Maltz*

To every man there comes in his lifetime that special moment when he is tapped on the shoulder and offered the chance to do a very special thing. What a tragedy if that moment finds him unprepared or unqualified for the work which would be his finest hour.

– *Winston Churchill*

Give me a stock clerk with a goal, and I will give you a man who will make history. Give me a man without a goal, and I will give you a stock clerk.

– *J.C. Penney*

You must get good at one of two things:
sowing in the spring or begging in the fall.
– *Jim Rohn*

Ask God's blessing on your work, but don't ask
him to do it for you.
– *Dame Flora Robson*

You can't aim a duck to death.
– *Gael Boardman*

Setting a goal is not the main thing. It is
deciding how you will go about achieving it
and staying with that plan.
– *Tom Landry*

Man cannot discover new oceans unless he has
the courage to lose sight of the shore.
– *Andre Gide*

If a man knows not what harbor he seeks, any
wind is the right wind.
– *Seneca*

You cannot escape the responsibility of
tomorrow by evading it today.
— *Abraham Lincoln*

Decisions without actions are worthless.
— *W. Clement Stone*

Success is based on imagination plus ambition
and the will to work.
— *Thomas Edison*

Progress always involves risk; you can't steal
second base and keep your foot on first.
— *Frederick Wilcox*

You can't build a reputation on what you are
going to do.
— *Henry Ford*

I skate to where the puck is going to be, not
where it is.
— *Wayne Gretzky*

If you can't win, make the fellow ahead of you break the record.
> — *Charles L. Tiblom*

Don't be afraid to take big steps. You can't cross a chasm in two jumps.
> — *David Lloyd George*

Behold the turtle. He makes progress only when he sticks his neck out.
> — *James B. Conant*

To read well, that is to read true books in a true spirit, is a noble exercise.
> — *Henry David Thoreau*

Never doubt that a small group of concerned citizens can change the world. Indeed, it is the only thing that ever has.
> — *Margaret Mead*

Let your hook always be cast; in the pool
where you least expect it, there will be fish.
— *Ovid*

All of us tend to put off living. We are all
dreaming of some magical rose garden over
the horizon, instead of enjoying the roses that
are blooming outside our windows today.
— *Dale Carnegie*

In any moment of decision the best thing you
can do is the right thing. The worst thing you
can do is nothing.
— *Theodore Roosevelt*

A knowledge of the path cannot be substituted
for putting one foot in front of the other.
— *M.C. Richards*

Swing at the strikes.
— *Yogi Berra*

The dictionary is the only place where success
comes before work.
— *Mark Twain*

Even if you're on the right track, you'll get run over if you just sit there.

— Will Rogers

The only thing necessary for the triumph of evil is for good men to do nothing.

— Edmund Burke

The great aim of education is not knowledge, but action.

— Anonymous

The man who doesn't read good books has no advantage over the man who can't read them.

— Mark Twain

Take a chance! All life is a chance. The man who goes the furthest is generally the one who is willing to do a dare. The 'sure thing' boat never gets far from shore.

— Dale Carnegie

THE PERSISTENCE CHOICE ...
LEARNING FROM FAILURE

Winners are committed to "hang in there"
long enough to win.

The choice of persistence is about setting a goal and "hanging in there" long enough to achieve it. It is about hurdling roadblocks and continuing your journey in spite of what life throws your way.

Most of the time success is achieved by those who want it most, create a plan to make it happen and are committed to persevere past their failures. Don't give up right before you are about to win.

We must all suffer from one of two pains: the pain of discipline or the pain of regret. The difference is discipline weighs ounces while regret weighs tons.

— *Jim Rohn*

When you come to the end of your rope, tie a knot and hang on.

— *Franklin Roosevelt*

Failure is delay, but not defeat. It is a temporary detour, not a dead-end street.

— *William Arthur Ward*

Develop success from failures. Discouragement and failure are two of the surest stepping stones to success.

— *Dale Carnegie*

Success … seems to be connected with action. Successful men keep moving. They make mistakes, but they don't quit.
— *Conrad Hilton*

If I had to select one quality, one personal characteristic that I regard as being most highly correlated with success, whatever the field, I would pick the trait of persistence. Determination. The will to endure to the end, to get knocked down seventy times and get up off the floor and say, "Here goes number seventy-one!"
— *Richard M. DeVos*

I have learned that success is to be measured not so much by the position that one has reached in life as by the obstacles which one has overcome while trying to succeed.
— *Booker T. Washington*

Men's best successes come after their disappointments.
— *Henry Ward Beecher*

The credit belongs to the man who is actually in the arena; whose face is marred by dust and sweat and blood; who strives valiantly; who errs and comes short again and again; who knows the great enthusiasms, the great devotions, and spends himself in a worthy cause; who, at the best, knows in the end the triumph of high achievement; and who, at the worst, if he fails, at least fails while daring greatly, so that his place shall never be with those cold and timid souls who know neither victory nor defeat.

— *Theodore Roosevelt*

Success is going from failure to failure without losing enthusiasm.

— *Winston Churchill*

Many of life's failures are people who did not realize how close they were to success when they gave up.

— *Thomas Edison*

Perseverance is not a long race; it is many short races one after another.

— *Walter Elliott*

You cannot measure a man by his failures. You must know what use he makes of them. What did they mean to him? What did he get out of them?

— *Orison Swett Marden*

The most essential factor is persistence — the determination never to allow your energy or enthusiasm to be dampened by the discouragement that must inevitably come.

— *James Whitcomb Riley*

A small trouble is like a pebble. Hold it too close to your eye and it fills the whole world and puts everything out of focus. Hold it at a proper distance and it can be examined and properly classified. Throw it at your feet and it can be seen in its true setting, just one more tiny bump on the pathway of life.

— *Celia Luce*

If you're willing to accept failure and learn from it, if you're willing to consider failure as a blessing in disguise and bounce back, you've got the potential of harnessing one of the most powerful success forces.

— Joseph Sugarman

Failure is, in a sense, the highway to success, as each discovery of what is false leads us to seek earnestly after what is true.

— John Keats

You gotta be before you can do, and you've gotta do before you can have.

— Zig Ziglar

Never, never, never, never … give in.

— Winston Churchill

It is not because things are difficult that we do not dare; it is because we do not dare that they are difficult.

— Seneca

Don't be afraid to fail. Don't waste energy trying to cover up failure. Learn from your failures and go on to the next challenge. It's OK to fail. If you're not failing, you're not growing.
— *H. Stanley Judd*

Not many people are willing to give failure a second opportunity. They fail once and it's all over. The bitter pill of failure … is often more than most people can handle … If you're willing to accept failure and learn from it, if you're willing to consider failure as a blessing in disguise and bounce back, you've got the potential of harnessing one of the most powerful success forces.
— *Joseph Sugarman*

One of the great discoveries a man makes, and one of his great surprises, is to find he can do what he was afraid he couldn't do.
— *Henry Ford*

Success seems to be largely a matter of hanging on after others have let go.
— *William Feather*

It may not be your fault for being down, but it is your fault for not getting up.
— *Steve Davis*

The person interested in success has to learn to view failure as a healthy, inevitable part of the process of getting to the top.
— *Joyce Brothers*

Nothing in the world can take the place of persistence. Talent will not. Nothing is more common than unsuccessful men with talent. Genius will not. Unrewarded genius is almost a proverb. Education will not. The world is full of educated derelicts. Persistence, determination and hard work make the difference.
— *Calvin Coolidge*

The biggest failure of all is the person that never tries.
— *Dr. Larry Kimsey*

Others can stop you temporarily — you are the only one who can do it permanently.
— *Zig Ziglar*

Life shrinks or expands in proportion to one's courage.
> — *Anais Nin*

———————

Ninety percent of those who fail are not actually defeated. They simply quit.
> — *Paul J. Meyer*

———————

You gain strength, experience and confidence by every experience where you really stop to look fear in the face … You must do the thing you cannot do.
> — *Eleanor Roosevelt*

———————

Discipline is the bridge between goals and accomplishment.
> — *Jim Rohn*

———————

The error of the past is the success of the future. A mistake is evidence that someone tried to do something.
> — *Anonymous*

———————

The greatest mistake you can make is to be continually fearing you will make one.
— *Elbert Hubbard*

Success ... seems to be connected with action. Successful people keep moving. They make mistakes, but they don't quit.
— *Conrad Hilton*

Consider it pure joy, my brothers, whenever you face trials of many kinds, because you know that the testing of your faith develops perseverance.
— *James 1:2-3*

I do not think there is any other quality so essential to success of any kind as the quality of perseverance. It overcomes almost everything, even nature.
— *John D. Rockefeller*

Failure is only the opportunity to more intelligently begin again.
— *Henry Ford*

Most people give up just when they're about to achieve success. They quit on the one-yard line. They give up at the last minute of the game one foot from a winning touchdown.
— *H. Ross Perot*

Experience is simply the name we give our mistakes.
— *Oscar Wilde*

In theory, there is no difference between theory and practice. In practice there is.
— *Yogi Berra*

There is no traffic jam on the extra mile.
— *Anonymous*

There is nothing so fatal to character as half-finished tasks.
— *David Lloyd George*

I am a slow walker, but I never walk backwards.
— *Abraham Lincoln*

Thousands of people have talent. The one and only thing that counts is: Do you have staying power?

— *Noel Coward*

We are what we repeatedly do. Excellence, then, is not an act but a habit.

— *Aristotle*

Effort only fully realizes its reward after a person refuses to quit.

— *Napoleon Hill*

The only person who is educated is the one who has learned how to learn … and change.

— *Carl Rogers*

Failure is success if we learn from it.

— *Malcolm Forbes*

Success is not forever and failure isn't fatal.

— *Don Shula*

Confidence doesn't come out of nowhere. It is a result of something ... hours and days and weeks and years of constant work and dedication.
— *Roger Staubach*

We should have no regrets. The past is finished. There is nothing to be gained by going over it. Whatever it gave us in the experiences it brought us was something we had to know.
— *Rebecca Beard*

Courage changes things for the better ... With courage, you can stay with something long enough to succeed at it — realizing that it usually takes two, three, or four times as long to succeed as you thought or hoped.
— *Earl Nightingale*

There are no easy businesses. Every single one is hard. Having perseverance means, most critically, persevering through failure. I love to talk about my successes, but the only way that I've ever learned anything is through failure.
— *Martin Cooper,*
inventor of the cell phone

THE ATTITUDE CHOICE ...
THE ENTHUSIASTIC APPROACH

Successful people typically demonstrate the courage to remain optimistic and search for the best – even in times of stress and uncertainty.

Your attitude is powerful. It can convince or discourage others who are watching you. A positive attitude can mean the difference between a survivor and a victim because it impacts every part of your life. It is the linchpin for successes and failures.

Your attitude – today, tomorrow and forever – is your choice. Choose wisely.

Knowledge is power, but enthusiasm pulls the switch.

— *Ivern Ball*

Wake up with a smile and go after life ... Live it, enjoy it, taste it, smell it, feel it.

— *Joe Knapp*

There's very little difference in people. But that little difference makes a big difference. The little difference is attitude. The BIG DIFFERENCE is whether it is positive or negative.

— *W. Clement Stone*

If you aren't fired with enthusiasm, you will be fired with enthusiasm.

— *Vince Lombardi*

Far away in the sunshine are my highest
inspirations. I may not reach them, but I can
look up and see the beauty, believe in them
and try to follow where they lead.
— *Louisa May Alcott*

Think enthusiastically about everything; but
especially about your job. If you do so, you'll put
a touch of glory in your life. If you love your job
with enthusiasm, you'll shake it to pieces.
— *Norman Vincent Peale*

Every man is enthusiastic at times. One man
has enthusiasm for thirty minutes, another man
has it for thirty days. But it is the man who has
it for thirty years who makes a success in life.
— *Edward B. Butler*

Think and feel yourself there! To achieve any
aim in life, you need to project the end-result …
Think of the elation, the satisfaction, the joy!
Carrying the ecstatic feeling will bring the
desired goal into view.
— *Grace Speare*

When you cease to dream you cease to live.
— *Malcolm Forbes*

He that expects nothing shall not be
disappointed, but he that expects much —
if he lives and uses that in hand day by day —
shall be full to running over.
— *Edgar Cayce*

An optimist may see a light where there is
none, but why must the pessimist always run
to blow it out?
— *Michel de Saint-Pierre*

If you want to be happy, put your effort into
controlling the sail, not the wind.
— *Anonymous*

An obvious fact about negative feelings is
often overlooked. They are caused by us, not
by exterior happenings. An outside event
presents the challenge, but we react to it. So
we must attend to the way we take things, not
to the things themselves.
— *Vernon Howard*

Use words to change your situation, not to describe it.

> – *Lee J. Colan*

A pessimist is a person who, regardless of the present, is disappointed in the future.

> – *John Maxwell*

An optimist sees an opportunity in every calamity; a pessimist sees a calamity in every opportunity.

> – *Winston Churchill*

Life is too short not to be happy and too long not to do well.

> – *Bryan Dodge*

The biggest quality in successful people, I think, is impatience with negative thinking … my feeling was even if it's as bad as I think it is, we'll make it work.

> – *Edward McCabe*

You will do foolish things, but do them with enthusiasm.

— *Sidonie Gabrielle Colette*

Ask yourself a question: Is my attitude worth catching?

— *Zig Ziglar*

The only thing we have to fear is fear itself — and possibly the bogeyman.

— *Pat Paulsen*

Happiness doesn't depend upon who you are or what you have; it depends solely upon what you think.

— *Dale Carnegie*

When you're looking at the sun, you see no shadows.

— *Helen Keller*

Sour grapes can ne'er make sweet wine.

— *Thomas Fuller*

Some people are always grumbling that roses
have thorns; I am thankful that thorns have roses.
— *Alphonse Karr*

Whatever is true, whatever is noble, whatever
is right, whatever is pure, whatever is lovely,
whatever is admirable — if anything is excellent
or praiseworthy — think about such things.
— *Philippians 4:8*

'I can't do it' never yet accomplished anything;
'I will try' has performed wonders.
— *George P. Burnham*

There are two days about which nobody
should ever worry, and these are yesterday
and tomorrow.
— *Robert Jones Burdette*

Change your thoughts and you change your world.
— *Norman Vincent Peale*

But a man who doesn't dream is like a man who doesn't sweat. He stores up a lot of poison.
— *Truman Capote*

Flaming enthusiasm, backed by horse sense and persistence, is the quality that most frequently makes for success.
— *Dale Carnegie*

Expect the best, plan for the worst, and prepare to be surprised.
— *Denis Waitley*

People who say it cannot be done should not interrupt those who are doing it.
— *Anonymous*

Years may wrinkle the skin, but to give up enthusiasm wrinkles the soul.
— *Samuel Ullman*

There has never been a great athlete who died not knowing what pain is.
— *Bill Bradley*

Change your thoughts and you change your world.
> — *Norman Vincent Peale*

A person has two legs and one sense of humor, and if faced with the choice, it's better to lose a leg.
> — *Charles Lindner*

A happy person is not a person in a certain set of circumstances, but rather a person with a certain set of attitudes.
> — *Hugh Downs*

Whether you think you can or think you can't, you're right.
> — *Benjamin Franklin*

Do not worry about tomorrow, for tomorrow will worry about itself. Each day has enough trouble of its own.
> — *Matthew 6:34*

Let us be of good cheer, remembering that the misfortunes hardest to bear are those which never happen.
— *James Russell Lowell*

Surround yourself with people who are optimistic and caring; it's one time when being 'surrounded' is a good thing.
— *Al Lucia*

A pessimist is one who makes difficulties of his opportunities. An optimist is one who makes opportunities of his difficulties.
— *Harry Truman*

Everything can be taken from a man but one thing: the last of the human freedoms — to choose one's attitude in any given set of circumstances, to choose one's own way.
— *Viktor Frankl*

Your living is determined not so much by
what life brings to you as by the attitude you
bring to life; not so much by what happens to
you as by the way your mind looks at what
happens.

— *John Homer Miller*

Virtually nothing on earth can stop a person
with a positive attitude who has his goal clearly
in sight.

— *Denis Waitley*

We must all wage an intense, lifelong battle
against the constant downward pull. If we relax,
the bugs and the weeds of negativity will move
into the garden and take away everything
of value.

— *Jim Rohn*

If one advances confidently in the direction of
his dreams, and endeavors to live a life which
he has imagined, he will meet with a success
unexpected in common hours.

— *Henry David Thoreau*

THE ADVERSITY CHOICE ...
CONQUERING DIFFICULT TIMES

Press on! Your most defining moment may arrive just when you feel surrounded by adversity.

At one time or another, everyone is confronted by adversity. The question we have to answer is, "How are we going to respond to the adversity we are facing?" Many times, adversity opens doors for us to explore new thoughts, ideas and solutions we would not have otherwise considered.

Whatever situation you are facing, press on with the presence of mind to explore workable alternatives to overcome adversity and move upward to the next level.

Within all of us are wells of thought and dynamos of energy which are not suspected until emergencies arise. Then, oftentimes, we find that it is comparatively simple to double or triple our former capacities and to amaze ourselves by the results achieved.

— *Thomas J. Watson*

We are continually faced with great opportunities brilliantly disguised as insolvable problems.

— *Lee Iacocca*

When it comes to problems and conflict, people who bury their heads in the sand will find that their backsides are exposed.

— *Ken Carnes*

The very greatest things – great thoughts,
discoveries, inventions – have usually been
nurtured in hardship, often pondered over in
sorrow, and at length established with difficulty.
— *Samuel Smiles*

Life is a series of experiences, each one of which
makes us bigger, even though sometimes it is
hard to realize this. For the world was built to
develop character, and we must learn that the
setbacks and griefs which we endure help us in
our marching onward.
— *Henry Ford*

Happiness does not come from doing easy work but from the afterglow of satisfaction that comes after the achievement of a difficult task that demanded our best.
— *Theodore I. Rubin*

Attach yourself to your passion, but not to your pain. Adversity is your best friend on the path to success.

— *Anonymous*

Adversity introduces a man to himself.

— *Anonymous*

In times like these, it helps to recall that there have always been times like these.

— *Paul Harvey*

There are no gains without pains.

— *Benjamin Franklin*

The rock that is an obstacle in the path of one person becomes a stepping stone in the path of another.

— *Anonymous*

This, too, shall pass.

— *William Shakespeare*

Regardless of how bleak the situation appears, there are alternatives that will help you move forward … if you choose to see them.
— *Chris Novak*

We must look for the opportunity in every difficulty instead of being paralyzed at the thought of the difficulty in every opportunity.
— *Walter E. Cole*

A wise man will make more opportunities than he finds.
— *Francis Bacon*

The measure of a man is not where he stands in moments of convenience, but where he stands in times of challenge and adversity.
— *Dr. Martin Luther King*

Successful people keep moving even when they are scared and have made mistakes … unsuccessful people quit before they have a chance to be successful.
— *Alice Adams*

What happens to a man is less significant than what happens within him.

— *Louis L. Mann*

Adversity causes some men to break, others to break records.

— *William Arthur Ward*

Tackling adversity means moving forward with the knowledge that some questions need action, not answers.

— *Chris Novak*

If things go wrong, don't go with them.

— *Roger Babson*

Trouble is opportunity in work clothes.

— *W. Clement Stone*

All rising to a great place is by a winding stair.

— *Abraham Lincoln*

Every winner has scars.
> — *Herbert Casson*

Things don't go wrong and break your heart
so you can become bitter and give up. They
happen to break you down and build you up
so you can be all that you were intended to be.
> — *Charlie "Tremendous" Jones*

Trouble will come soon enough, and when
he does come receive him as pleasantly as
possible … the more amiably you greet him,
the sooner he will go away.
> — *Artemus Ward*

Obstacles are those frightful things you see
when you take your eyes off your goals.
> — *Anonymous*

The world isn't interested in the storms you
encountered but whether you brought in
the ship.
> — *Raul Armesto*

Life is a series of problems. Do we want to moan about them or solve them?
— *M. Scott Peck*

———————

It's a misnomer that our talents make us a success. They help, but it's not what we do well that enables us to achieve in the long run. It's what we do wrong and how we correct it that ensures our long-lasting success.
— *Bernie Marcus*

———————

There will be more problems. There's no escaping it — it's a fact of life. The question is, are you going to be proactive and take action to avert a crisis, or are you going to do nothing and hope things turn out okay?
— *Stephen Krempl*

———————

PART THREE

THE INVESTMENT CHOICES ...
THE PROFIT OF SUCCESS.

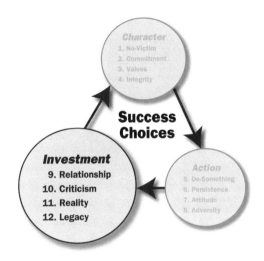

"Make every thought, every fact, that comes
into your mind pay you a profit. Make it work
and produce for you. Think of things not
as they are but as they might be.
Don't merely dream – but create!"

– Robert Collier

THE RELATIONSHIP CHOICE ...
CONNECTING WITH SUCCESS

Teamwork is connected independence.

What would life be without relationships?

Healthy relationships – those that are mutually caring and giving – are necessary for personal success. Everyone needs someone to learn from and share ideas. These relationships offer understanding when we fail, confidence when we're in doubt and celebration as we go through life. They also allow us opportunities to give, to mentor and to share.

Take time to nurture and appreciate the relationships that make a difference in your life.

Even the Lone Ranger didn't do it alone.
— *Harvey MacKay*

Personal relationships are the fertile soil from which all advancement, all success, all achievement in real life grows.
— *Ben Stein*

Life is not so short but that there is always time enough for courtesy.
— *Ralph Waldo Emerson*

I believe that you can get everything in life you want if you will just help enough other people get what they want.

– Zig Ziglar

What makes a truly successful executive is not intelligence, education, lifestyle, or background. The principal factor that determines an executive's success is his or her ability to deal with people.

– Anonymous

When weighing the faults of others, be careful not to put your thumb on the scale.

– Anonymous

I can live for two months on a good compliment.

– Mark Twain

Alone we can do so little; together we can do so much.

– Helen Keller

When nobody around you seems to measure up, it's time to check your yardstick.
— *Bill Lemley*

Remember: We become who we spend time with. The quality of a person's life is most often a direct reflection of the expectations of their peer group. Choose your friends well.
— *Anthony Robbins*

Success depends on the support of other people. The only hurdle between you and what you want to be is the support of others.
— *David Joseph Schwartz*

Relationships are built on trust and respect, cemented together with shared experiences.
— *Valerie Sokolosky*

You will become like the five people you associate with the most. This can be either a blessing or a curse.
— *Billy Cox*

You can make more friends in two months by becoming interested in other people than you can in two years by trying to get other people interested in you.

– Dale Carnegie

Do not be misled: 'Bad company corrupts good character.'
– 1 Corinthians 15:33

Thinking to get at once all the gold the goose could give, he killed it and opened it only to find – nothing.

– Aesop

There is no such thing as a self-made man. You will reach your goals only with the help of others.

– George Shinn

Recipe for having friends: Be one.

– Elbert Hubbard

It has been my experience that folks that have
no vices have very few virtues.
— *Abraham Lincoln*

Always be a first-rate version of yourself, instead
of a second-rate version of somebody else.
— *Judy Garland*

It takes so little to make people happy. Just a
touch, if we know how to give it, just a word
fitly spoken, a slight readjustment of some bolt
or pin or bearing in the delicate machinery of
a soul.
— *Frank Crane*

He has achieved success who has lived well, laughed often, and loved much.
— *Anonymous*

He that lieth down with dogs, shall rise up
with fleas.
— *Benjamin Franklin*

It's the things in common that make relationships enjoyable, but it's the little differences that make them interesting.
— *Todd Ruthman*

After the game, the king and the pawn go into the same box.
— *Italian proverb*

Loyalty is something you give regardless of what you get back. In giving loyalty, you're getting more loyalty; and out of loyalty flow other great qualities.
— *Charlie "Tremendous" Jones*

Do nothing out of selfish ambition or vain conceit, but in humility consider others better than yourselves. Each of you should look not only to your own interests, but also to the interests of others.
— *Philippians 2: 3-4*

We must learn to live together as brothers or perish together as fools.
— *Martin Luther King, Jr.*

It is surprising how much you can accomplish if you don't care who gets the credit.
— *Abraham Lincoln*

If there is any one secret of success, it lies in the ability to get the other person's point of view and see things from that person's angle as well as from your own.
— *Henry Ford*

One of the secrets of a long and fruitful life is to forgive everybody everything every night before going to bed.
— *Bernard Baruch*

The most important single ingredient in the formula of success is knowing how to get along with people.
— *Theodore Roosevelt*

So in everything, do to others what you would have them do to you.
— *Matthew 7:12*

Somebody says, 'Well, I can't be concerned about other people. About the best I can do is to take care of myself.' Well, then you will always be poor.

— *Jim Rohn*

Our rewards in life will always be in exact proportion to the amount of consideration we show toward others.

— *Earl Nightingale*

Few things in the world are more powerful than a positive push. A smile. A word of optimism and hope. A 'you can do it' when things are tough.

— *Richard M. DeVos*

None of us is more important than the rest of us.

— *Ray Kroc*

It marks a big step in your development when you come to realize that other people can help you do a better job than you could do alone.
— *Andrew Carnegie*

Coming together is a beginning; keeping together is progress; working together is success.
— *Henry Ford*

The most important thing in communication is to hear what isn't being said.
— *Peter F. Drucker*

One person seeking glory doesn't accomplish much. Success is a result of people pulling together to meet common goals.
— *John Maxwell*

Do not sit long with a sad friend. When you go to a garden do you look at the weeds? Spend more time with the roses and jasmines.
— *Jelaluddin Rumi*

The golden rule is of no use whatsoever unless you realize that it is your move.

> — *Dr. Frank Crane*

Relationships of trust depend on our willingness to look not only to our own interests, but also the interests of others.

> — *Peter Farquharson*

Three things in human life are important: The first is to be kind. The second is to be kind. And the third is to be kind.

> — *Henry James*

Never fail to know that if you are doing all the talking, you are boring somebody.

> — *Helen Gurley Brown*

There is no exercise better for the heart than reaching down and lifting people up.

> — *John Andrew Holmes*

Example is not the main thing in influencing others. It is the only thing.
> – *Albert Schweitzer*

———————

Nice guys may appear to finish last, but usually they are running in a different race.
> – *Ken Blanchard*

———————

THE CRITICISM CHOICE ...
TOUGH LEARNING

Accept constructive criticism as a gift ...
a learning tool that teaches us lessons
throughout our life.

Most people profess to have the ability to accept constructive criticism. The test is to make an immediate determination whether negative comments are truly constructive.

Without a doubt, success breeds criticism from all corners ... and we need criticism to reach our full potential. The trick is to embrace constructive, sincere criticism as teaching tools from which we can polish our skills and ideas. Criticism is a gift ... learn from it!

The trouble with most of us is that we would rather be ruined by praise than saved by criticism.
— *Norman Vincent Peale*

Remember, if people talk behind your back, it only means you're two steps ahead.
— *Fannie Flagg*

Criticism is the windows and chandeliers of art: it illuminates the enveloping darkness in which art might otherwise rest only vaguely discernible, and perhaps altogether unseen.
— *George Jean Nathan*

Coaches have to watch for what they don't want to see and listen for what they don't want to hear.

> *— John Madden*

Success is simply a matter of luck — ask any failure.

> *— Earl Wilson*

Eating my words has never given me indigestion.
> *— Winston Churchill*

Life asks us to make measurable progress in reasonable time. That's why they make those fourth-grade chairs so small — so you won't fit in them at age twenty-five!

> *— Jim Rohn*

He that won't be counseled can't be helped.
> *— Benjamin Franklin*

We can't learn anything new until we can admit that we don't already know everything.
— *Erwin G. Hall*

Listen to advice and accept instruction, and in the end you will be wise.
— *Proverbs 19:20*

Feedback is the breakfast of champions.
— *Rick Tate*

He has the right to criticize who has the heart to help.
— *Abraham Lincoln*

The healthy and strong individual is the one who asks for help when he needs it. Whether he's got an abscess on his knee, or in his soul.
— *Rona Barrett*

Courage is what it takes to stand up and speak; courage is also what it takes to sit down and listen.
— *Anonymous*

THE REALITY CHOICE ...
FACING TRUTH

---

*Courage is moving forward ... even through
the path of most resistance.*

Reality can be defined as the truth –
the real nature of something – the facts.
A key element to success is discovering
and then facing reality – the reality of
our opportunities, corporate culture, our
talents ... and more.

Choosing to search for the truth and having the courage to confront the hard realities will pay dividends to your career. You'll find the road to success a little straighter, the challenges less overwhelming and fewer surprises along the way.

Face reality as it is ... not as you wish it to be.
— *Jack Welch*

It is the chiefest point of happiness that a man is willing to be what he is.
— *Desiderius Erasmus*

Tomorrow's greatest leaders are those with the courage to face reality and help the people around them face reality.
— *Ronald Heifetz*

When your heart speaks, take good notes.
— *Anonymous*

The only certain means of success is to render more and better service than is expected of you, no matter what your task may be.
— *Og Mandino*

Do not take life too seriously. You will never get out of it alive.
— *Elbert Hubbard*

There is nothing so powerful as truth — and often nothing so strange.
— *Daniel Webster*

Personally I am always ready to learn, although I do not always like being taught.
— *Winston Churchill*

Don't paint stripes on your back if you're not a zebra. Focus on building upon your unique abilities.
— *Lee J. Colan*

You might well remember that nothing can bring you success but yourself.

— *Napoleon Hill*

Either you deal with what is the reality, or you can be sure that the reality is going to deal with you.

— *Alex Haley*

Truth is not beautiful, neither is it ugly. Why should it be either? Truth is truth …

— *Owen C. Middleton*

No matter what you want to accomplish, you are going to need more knowledge than you have now.

— *Brian Tracy*

The success combination in business is: Do what you do better … and: Do more of what you do ….

— *David Joseph Schwartz*

Accept everything about yourself – I mean everything. You are you and that is the beginning and the end – no apologies, no regrets.
— *Clark Moustakas*

You don't know what you don't know. Open your mind to discover possibilities that may not be obvious at the time.
— *Vince Poscente*

Your big opportunity may be right where you are now.
— *Napoleon Hill*

Once a person says, 'This is who I really am, what I am all about, what I was really meant to do,' it is easier to decide how to spend one's time.
— *David Viscott*

No man, for any considerable period, can wear one face to himself, and another to the multitude, without finally getting bewildered as to which may be the true.
— *Nathaniel Hawthorne*

There is a certain kind of comfort in knowing the truth ... even if it is tough to face.
— *Stephen Krempl*

The golden opportunity you are seeking is in yourself. It is not in your environment; it is not in luck or chance, or the help of others; it is in yourself alone.
— *Orison Swett Marden*

Growth begins when we start to accept our own weakness.
— *Jean Vanier*

Happy the man who early learns the wide chasm that lies between his wishes and his powers.
— *Johann von Goethe*

Learn from the mistakes of others — you can't live long enough to make them all yourself.
— *Martin Vanbee*

To act is easy; to think is hard.
— *Johann von Goethe*

Embrace the truths ... not what you want to
believe, but what is ... and re-evaluate regularly.
— *Alice Adams*

Never try to catch two frogs with one hand.
— *Chinese proverb*

The tragedy of life doesn't lie in not reaching
your goal. The tragedy lies in having no goal
to reach. It isn't a calamity to die with dreams
unfilled, but it is a calamity not to dream. It
is not disgrace to reach the stars, but it is a
disgrace to have no stars to reach for. Not
failure, but low aim, is a sin.
— *Benjamin Mays*

Your greatest liability is the one you are
unaware of.
— *Lee J. Colan*

Too many people overvalue what they are not and undervalue what they are.
— *Malcolm Forbes*

Never undertake anything for which you wouldn't have the courage to ask the blessings of heaven.

— Georg Christoph Lichtenberg

The best place to find a helping hand is at the end of your own arm.

— Swedish proverb

We either make ourselves miserable, or we make ourselves strong. The amount of work is the same.

— Carlos Castaneda

If you want to make a silk purse out of a sow's ear, it helps to start with a silk sow.

— Steve Ventura

Life is not the way it's supposed to be. It's the way it is. The way you cope with it is what makes the difference.

— Virginia Satir

It's not enough that we do our best; sometimes we have to do what's required.
> – *Winston Churchill*

Make it a rule of life never to regret and never look back. Regret is an appalling waste of energy; you can't build on it; it is good only for wallowing in.
> – *Katherine Mansfield*

When one door closes, another door opens; but we often look so long and regretfully upon the closed door that we do not see the ones which open.
> – *Alexander Graham Bell*

It's not the will to win, but the will to prepare to win that makes the difference.
> – *Bear Bryant*

The time to repair the roof is when the sun is shining.
> – *John F. Kennedy*

No matter who you are or what your age may be, if you want to achieve permanent, sustaining success, the motivation that will drive you toward that goal must come from within.
— *Paul J. Meyer*

The truth is incontrovertible. Malice may attack it and ignorance may deride it, but in the end, there it is.
— *Winston Churchill*

The great enemy of the truth is very often not the lie — deliberate, contrived and dishonest; but the myth — persistent, persuasive and unrealistic.
— *John F. Kennedy*

Life is 10 percent what you make it, and 90 percent how you take it.
— *Irving Berlin*

The best preparation for a better life next year is a full, complete, harmonious, joyous life this year.
— *Thomas Dreier*

If you're never scared or embarrassed or hurt,
it means you never take any chances.
— *Julia Sorel*

A man reaps what he sows.
— *Galatians 6:7*

What we call the beginning is often an end.
And to make an end is to make a beginning.
The end is where we start from.
— *T.S. Eliot*

It takes time to succeed because success is
merely the natural reward of taking time to do
anything well.
— *Joseph Ross*

What you are afraid to do is a clear indicator of the next thing you need to do.
— *Anonymous*

If you want a quality, act as if you already have it.
— *William James*

Worry is a futile thing; it's somewhat like a rocking chair. Although it keeps you occupied, it doesn't get you anywhere.
— *Anonymous*

Nature gave men two ends — one to sit on, and one to think with. Ever since then man's success or failure has been dependent on the one he used most.
— *George R. Kirkpatrick*

THE LEGACY CHOICE …
YOUR GIFT

---

*There are reasons why hearses don't have
luggage racks! Your legacy will be
what you leave others.*

The heart of every legacy is what an
individual has given back – to their
co-workers, their organization, their
family and their community. Your legacy
is your imprint on the future that lasts
long after your last breath.

Begin today to give back. Your career may be an unparalleled success, but your legacy will distinguish you most and provide the greatest meaning to your life.

In everyone's life, at some time, our inner fire goes out. It is then burst into flame by an encounter with another human being. We should all be thankful for those people who rekindle the inner spirit.
— Albert Schweitzer

In this world it is not what we take up, but what we give up, that makes us rich.
— Henry Ward Beecher

Nobody who ever gave his best regretted it.
— George Halas

Aim at heaven and you get earth thrown in; aim at earth and you get neither.
— C.S. Lewis

It is one of the most beautiful compensations of life, that no man can sincerely try to help another without helping himself.

— *Ralph Waldo Emerson*

The way we act is the way we teach.

— *Vince Poscente*

How far you go in life depends on you being tender with the young, compassionate with the aged, sympathetic with the striving and tolerant of the weak and the strong. Because someday in life you will have been all of these.

— *George Washington Carver*

We must give more in order to get more. It is the generous giving of ourselves that produces the generous harvest.

— *Orison Swett Marden*

When you share, the remainder multiplies and grows.

— *W. Clement Stone*

The best portion of a good man's life: his little nameless unremembered acts of kindness and of love.

— *William Wordsworth*

Seize every moment and passionately pursue life by being the very best you can be. No looking back. No regrets!

— *Ken Carnes*

I touch the future. I teach.

— *Christa McAuliffe*

For everyone who exalts himself will be humbled, and he who humbles himself will be exalted.

— *Luke 14:11*

Generous people are rarely mentally ill people.

— *Dr. Karl Menninger*

If you can't feed a hundred people, then feed just one.
> — *Mother Teresa*

We make a living from what we get; we make a life from what we give.
> — *Winston Churchill*

It is more blessed to give than to receive.
> — *Acts 20:35*

Give light, and darkness will disappear of itself.
> — *Desiderius Erasmus*

I don't know what your destiny will be, but one thing I do know: the only ones among you who will be really happy are those who have sought and found how to serve.
> — *Albert Schweitzer*

The best thing about giving of ourselves is that what we get is always better than what we give. The reaction is greater than the action.
> — *Orison Swett Marden*

A teacher affects eternity.
> – *Henry Brooks Adams*

Sharing makes you bigger than you are. The more you pour out, the more life will be able to pour in.
> – *Jim Rohn*

The best way to find yourself is to lose yourself in the service of others.
> – *Mahatma Gandhi*

There are two ways of spreading light: to be the candle or the mirror that reflects it.
> – *Edith Wharton*

We all leave footprints in the sand. The question is, will we be a big heel, or a great soul?
> – *Anonymous*

Plant a kernel of wheat and you reap a pint; plant a pint and you reap a bushel. Always the law works to give you back more than you give.
> – *Anthony Norvell*

You only get to keep what you give away.
— *Sheldon Kopp*

Sharing what you have is more important than what you have.
— *Albert M. Wells, Jr.*

When you were born, you cried and the world rejoiced. Live your life in such a manner that when you die the world cries and you rejoice.
— *Old Indian saying*

Give and it shall be given to you. A good measure, pressed down, shaken together and running over, will be poured into your lap. For with the measure you use, it will be measured to you.
— *Luke 6:38*

Don't curse the darkness — light a candle.
— *Chinese proverb*

Do all the good you can, by all the means you can, in all the ways you can, in all the places you can, at all the times you can, to all the people you can, as long as ever you can.

— *John Wesley*

We cannot hold a torch to light another's path without brightening our own.

— *Ben Sweetland*

We were meant to give our lives away. Focus on living your legacy instead of worrying about leaving it.

— *Lee J. Colan*

It is not what we leave our kids; it's what we leave within them that counts.

— *Valerie Sokolosky*

You cannot hold on to anything good. You must be continually giving – and getting. You cannot hold on to your seed. You must sow it – and reap anew. You cannot hold on to riches. You must use them and get other riches in return.

— *Robert Collier*

INSPIRATIONAL PASSAGES
FROM THE BIBLE

I believe that the greatest words ever written are recorded in the Bible. It has been the foundation for good choices in my life. Here are some of my favorite passages that have provided me strength and encouragement.

James 1:12 *Blessed is the man who perseveres under trial, because when he has stood the test, he will receive the crown of life that God has promised to those that love Him.*

Psalms 27:14 *Wait on the Lord: be of good courage, and He shall strengthen thine heart.*

Isaiah 42:16 *I will lead the blind by ways they have not known, along unfamiliar paths I will guide them; I will turn the darkness into light before them and make the rough places smooth. These things I will do; I will not forsake them.*

1 Peter 4:16 *If you suffer as a Christian, do not be ashamed, but praise God that you bear His name.*

Philippians 4:10 *I have learned to be content whatever the circumstances.*

Philippians 4:13 *I can do everything through Him who gives me strength.*

Philippians 4:19 *And my God will meet all of your needs according to His glorious riches in Christ Jesus.*

Hebrews 10:36 *You need to persevere so that when you have done the will of God, you will receive what He has promised.*

1 Timothy 6:17 *Command those who are rich in his present world not to be arrogant nor to put their hope in wealth, which is so uncertain, but to put their hope in God, who richly provides us with everything for our enjoyment.*

Proverbs 3:5-6   *Trust in the Lord with all your heart and lean not on your own understanding; in all your ways acknowledge Him, and He will make your paths straight.*

Joshua 1:9   *Have I not commanded you? Be strong and courageous. Do not be terrified, do not be discouraged, for the Lord your God will be with you wherever you go.*

Psalm 127:1 (KJV)   *Except the Lord build the house, they labor in vain that build it.*

1 Corinthians 10:13   *No temptation has seized you except what is common to man. And God is faithful; He will not let you be tempted beyond what you can bear. But when you are tempted, He will also provide a way out so that you can stand up under it.*

1 Corinthians 9:24   *Do you know that in a race all the runners run, but only one gets the prize? Run in such a way as to get the prize.*

Galatians 6:8-9   *The one who sows to please his sinful nature, from that nature will reap destruction; the one who sows to please the Spirit, from the Spirit will reap eternal life. Let us not become weary in doing good, for at the proper time we will reap a harvest if we do not give up.*

Philippians 3:13–14 *But one thing I do! Forgetting what is behind and straining toward what is ahead, I press on toward the goal to win the prize for which God has called me heavenward in Christ Jesus.*

2 Timothy 1:12 *That is why I am suffering as I am. Yet, I am not ashamed, because I know whom I have believed, and am convinced that He is able to guard what I have entrusted to Him for that day.*

Psalm 56:3 *When I am afraid, I will trust in you.*

1 Corinthians 16:13 *Be on your guard; stand firm in the faith; be men of courage; be strong. Do everything in love.*

Isaiah 40:31 *But those who hope in the Lord will renew their strength. They will soar on wings like eagles, they will run and not grow weary, they will walk and not faint.*

Psalm 46:1 *God is our refuge and strength, an ever present help in trouble.*

2 Chronicles 26:5 *As long as he sought the Lord, God gave him success.*

Isaiah 54:10 *Though the mountains be shaken and the hills be removed, yet my unfailing love for you will not be shaken nor my covenant of peace be removed, says the Lord, who has compassion on you.*

2 Timothy 2:15 *Do your best to present yourself to God as one approved, a workman who does not need to be ashamed and who correctly handles the word of truth.*

Romans 15:13 *May the God of hope fill you with all joy and peace as you trust in Him, so that you may overflow with hope by the power of the Holy Spirit.*

John 14:27 *Peace I leave with you; my peace I give you. I do not give to you as the world gives. Do not let your hearts be troubled and do not be afraid.*

ACKNOWLEDGEMENTS

Anyone who compiles quotations is faced with questions and concerns about accuracy. I have made every effort to attribute the quotes to the appropriate sources as accurately as possible. For those quotations that we could not verify the original source, we labeled it anonymous.

Quotations in this book are taken from the following and other books:

CornerStone Leadership Collection of Quotations, CornerStone, Texas, 2006

Great Quotes from Great Leaders, Great Quotations Publishing, Illinois, 1990

Leadership Smarts by Ken Blanchard, Honor Books, Colorado, 2004

Life's Greatest Lessons, Fireside Books, New York, 2003

The 100 Simple Secrets of Successful People, HarperCollins, New York, 2001

The Best of Success, Great Quotations Publishing, Illinois, 1988

The Book of Positive Quotations, Gramercy Books, New York, 1999

The Right Moment, William E. Hyche, Common Good Press, Texas, 2001

The Treasury of Quotes by Jim Rohn, Jim Rohn International, Dallas, Texas, 1994

The Wit and Wisdom of Abraham Lincoln, Gramercy Books, New York, 1996

The Wit and Wisdom of Benjamin Franklin, Gramercy Books, New York, 1995

The Wit and Wisdom of Mark Twain, Dover Publications, New York, 1999

The Wit and Wisdom of Winston Churchill, HarperCollins, New York, 1994

You Can't Afford the Luxury of a Negative Thought, Prelude, California, 1989

Zig Ziglar's Favorite Quotations, Great Quotations, Illinois, 1989

Unless otherwise indicated, all Scripture quotations are taken from the HOLY BIBLE, NEW INTERNATIONAL VERSION®, copyright © 1973, 1978, 1984, by International Bible Society. Used by permission of Zondervan Publishing House. All rights reserved.

Thank you for taking the time to read my favorite quotations. My desire is that these words of wisdom will be encouraging to you and a source for inspiration, today and tomorrow.

Enjoy life's journey!

David Cottrell
www.CornerStoneLeadership.com

Thank you for reading *David Cottrell's Collection of Favorite Quotations*. We hope it has assisted you in your quest for personal and professional growth.

CornerStone Leadership is committed to provide new and enlightening products to organizations worldwide. Our mission is to fuel knowledge with practical resources that will accelerate your team's productivity, success and job satisfaction!

Best wishes for your continued success.

To order additional copies of this book, and for additional products and resources, please call 1.888.789.5323 or visit www.CornerStoneLeadership.com

CornerStone
Leadership Institute
www.CornerStoneLeadership.com

*Start a crusade in your organization –
have the courage to learn, the vision to lead,
and the passion to share.*